I0697660

INTEGRITY

HOW TO SURVIVE TO A MULTINATIONAL

DAVID GRAÇA

ISBN: 9798878828529

David is a citizen of the world, born between France and Portugal, with a master's degree in aerospace engineering. With over two decades of procurement and supply chain experience, he has explored the professional world from France to Spain.

His recent turn in life, after a significant work experience, leads him to fulfill his dream of writing. This book is the culmination of his passion for reading and an opportunity to share lessons from his career and life.

Acknowledgments

To my two unwavering pillars, to the two women who have taught me to value life's most precious treasures:

To my grandmother, whose love and wisdom have illuminated my path since I was a child. Your warmth and infinite patience have guided me in moments of darkness, and your legacy of values will live on my heart forever. Thank you for being my source of inspiration.

To my mother, whose strength, unconditional love and solid principles have molded me into the human being I am today. Your lessons on the importance of integrity, respect and honesty have been a beacon in my life. I am grateful for every sacrifice and every smile you have shared with me.

To both of you, I owe my eternal gratitude and my commitment to continue living a life full of values and love. Your teachings shine in me and continue to guide my steps in this journey called life.

Finally, I want to thank you from the bottom of my heart! Especially you, dear reader, for taking the time to immerse yourself in the pages of my first literary work. Your support means the world to me, thank you!

Index

The secret of happiness is to do what you love.
The secret to success is to love what you do.

Author unknown

The secret of happiness is not always doing what you want,
but always wanting what you do.

Tolstoy

I.   Implementation of Values

"Fuck!" I exclaimed.

It was an April afternoon, shortly after Easter. We had rarely had such a mild temperature in Paris in some time. However, as we approached Charles-de-Gaulle airport, the temperature became more aggressive, creating an electric atmosphere that gave me goose bumps.

We were picking up a family friend who was returning from Portugal after a week's vacation to build the house of his dreams, thanks to his hard work over many years in a country that wasn't his own, all for a better life the day he should return home definitively when he would be retired.

It was in 1991 and I was about two years away from finishing high school, not knowing what subjects to choose for my future since I was a child. I was sure that my future would be surrounded by scientific subjects, each one more exciting than the other, instead of economics and law. My instincts alerted me that legal professions were complex because of the responsibility they require. Court became a nightmare when I remembered my desire to be a lawyer. I did not want to risk defending a criminal who had killed his entire family. The feeling of discomfort and fear of this profession was increasing with the progressive drop in temperature.

Being a scientist was the solution, but in which specialty? The medical profession crossed my mind slightly, but the narrowed selection made me forget it quickly. Until that spring evening, as we drove into the airport parking lot, a metallic giant was about to land on one of its lighted runways allowing the airline pilot to land quietly without jerks or sudden braking. A technological giant that defied all laws of gravity with elegance, charisma and enthusiasm.

Open-mouthed and incredulous at such a beast, I fell in love.

"What's wrong?" my father asked.

"I already know what I want to do in the next few years, I know how I can thrive as I work through my career," I replied.

"Really? And what is it?" my father asked again.

"Airline pilot," I replied still surprised.

Faced with a father who feared that I would become demotivated a few years later, because of the difficulty of studying to become an airline pilot, I showed him my confidence because I was sure that this was the direction I should take.

From 1993 to 1996, I spent three long years studying at the University of Pierre and Marie Curie in the heart of Paris, with the aspiration of becoming an airline pilot. I invested so much effort, only to realize in the home stretch that it would be impossible for me to fly a commercial airplane due to the early onset of a cataract when I was barely 20 years old. Although I experienced sadness, I felt proud that I would have had the chance to make it if my genetics had allowed me to do so. On the advice of a college friend who was enrolled in a business school in my hometown, Levallois-Perret, located in the Hauts-de-Seine and bordering Paris, I decided to change course.

In fact, the building in front of his school was a private school, training future engineers for transportation subjects such as aeronautics, automobile, railroad and space specialties.

The private school was accepting applications for new students until the following day at six o'clock in the evening. Considering my passion, I was able to write my cover letter to proceed my application in a record time of twelve hours.

The effort was rewarded from the moment I was admitted and left with my diploma in hand four years after my enrollment, in July 2000. While many of my classmates were debating which engineering major to pursue due to the untold number of subjects we assimilated during our degree, I was already clear about my direction. Although my creative and extravagant nature in everyday social life steered me towards a commercial career from 2000 to 2003, I managed to change course with great success, in 2003, when I realized that I could no longer sell the flagship product of my first company because I didn't believe in it. It was then that I decided to change direction and dive into the fascinating world of procurement and supply chains.

It was in this area where I accumulated more and more experience with the goal of joining the renowned aerospace Multinational and prosper in my career. After eight years since the end of my engineering studies, I achieved my goal by being hired by the Multinational of my most ambitious dreams in December 2008.

The Multinational was still young when I joined it. Over the next fifteen years, numerous changes were implemented to harmonize the operational processes of the different entities acquired by the Multinational. These changes not only provided me with training opportunities and experience, but also enriched my perspective on an international level, interacting with various companies both locally and globally. Although a lot of energy was invested and mistakes made, what better way to mature and grow old with time than doing what you love?

However, greed is to humans what the plague is to death. It chases you everywhere, setting the standards of modern life, and no one really knows where they come from or who implements them. Modern capitalism pushes you down a path you don't necessarily understand. That's why, after some insider trading and prohibited sales in embargoed countries, the Multinational is red-flagged and on the verge of being banned internationally. At that time, it was imperative to react quickly to address the situation, but, above all, it was crucial to define corrective and preventive measures to prevent this from happening again.

To achieve this, the Multinational established a code of conduct for all its employees with the aim of transforming its image at a global level. This code is based on values that no employee can deviate from without a legitimate reason. Six values guide this code, inspired by our volatile, uncertain, complex, and ambiguous world, and are broken down as follows:

1. Respect
2. Customer Focus
3. We Are One
4. Creativity
5. Reliability
6. Integrity

Values are to people what strategy is to business. They provide a shared language to achieve a common goal, so that the expected behavior generates a sense of belonging and identification with the Multinational, further integrating it into the market. The definition, implementation, and collective adoption of these values by all employees would facilitate to:

- Simplify complexity,
- Create a shared identity,
- Provide an Ethical Act to all its internal and external customers,
- Create a solid foundation for an even stronger corporate culture.

Identification and solidity are achieved only when all collaborators respect the internal and external rules of the Multinational, without exceptions, even when the outcome of a project seems more complex when adapted to our values. I prided myself on possessing all the values, well, perhaps with one small exception (that fascinating touch of creativity), courtesy of the multicultural upbringing I received over the years. As they say, dogs don't usually breed cats, and I must admit with all certainty: genetics is precise. My upbringing was like a balanced cocktail between paternal tutelage in the first half of my childhood and the wisdom of my maternal grandmother in the second half, providing me with a constant education without discrepancies on either side. How lucky I am!

I did not hesitate then to join the working group within the Multinational to explain, promote and instill values in all professions and functions. In the end, we formed a beautiful and big family.

How naive I was!

II.   Respect

Respect is the fundamental pillar, the foundation on which all values are built. To achieve this principle, it is imperative to adopt a zero-tolerance attitude towards unethical behavior and non-compliance, in order to preserve the culture rooted in the Multinational and ensure the delivery of quality products, on time and full compliant to external customer needs.

At the beginning of 2020, my manager had to change position to assume greater responsibilities within the Multinational due to his well-deserved promotion. It was this manager who gave me the opportunity to expand my skills and competencies on an international level by integrating me into his team based in Seville, Spain, in November 2015. Despite not speaking the language of the country, which was completely unfamiliar to me, having only crossed it on a handful of occasions or summer trips, these trips used to serve as a crucial encounter for Portuguese emigrants in France. For them, these trips represented a vital connection with their loved ones, whom they had not seen for a year. The "Saudade" enveloped them with intensity, transforming a people known for their joy of life into one more melancholic and distrustful towards life.

Our team found itself under new management when it passed from Spanish to German hands. This change was made in order to diversify the culture over the years and to comply with the agreements signed in 2000 between the governments of France, Germany, Spain and the United

Kingdom. These agreements sought to strengthen the European Union to cope more effectively with growing global competition. This trend had intensified since the 90's with the arrival of digital technology and the sale of certain mechanical technologies in Asia in the second decade of the 2000's.

The transition to his successor, Mike, was quite smooth; in fact, he insisted on having one-on-one meetings with each team member to get to know us better. Although my first impression was more of his observation than his active interaction. However, my concerns were not evident until, at the team meeting on the Monday following his arrival, our direct manager informed us that Mike wanted his team to use up their vacation days before December 31, 2020. This, of course, created a social conflict, as the Multinational's agreement stated that vacation could be taken until June 30 of the following year, in 2021.

A slight expression of disapproval crossed my face when I heard this directive, as it seemed contrary to respect for our rights and autonomy in choosing the private lives of team members. However, I decided not to give it too much importance at the time, since I was used to enjoy all my vacation before the end of each calendar year.

My move to Seville in 2015 was a painful process, partly due to the change of my French employment contract to a Spanish one. This change involved the liquidation of all the vacation days accumulated over the previous seven years in my time savings account, to which every worker in France has his or her labor right, and which were paid in one lump sum at the end of my contract. Paradoxically, this liquidation resulted in me leaving more money in the French Treasury than I brought back to Spain as cash or savings, although I still do not have a full understanding of the concept of personal savings.

Months later, an unexpected event occurred: my grandmother passed away in Portugal during my summer vacation. This gave me the right to take four extra days off to organize her funeral, since she lived in a different country. However, this event coincided with a critical moment in the procurement department and supply chain. We were in the midst of a crisis at the end of the year, struggling to complete the purchase orders and deliveries planned for the current year without exceeding the Multinational's annual budget. This situation was made even more challenging by the fact that we were in the post-pandemic stage and 2020 had not been economically favorable.

In addition, I was already managing numerous projects simultaneously, making it impossible to fulfill my internal client requests. This went against the most fundamental corporate value: the focus on customer satisfaction, a commitment I could not maintain if I reduced those four days off in the way Mike wanted. This created a conflict of interest between the Multinational's policy and that of the new leader.

III.   Customer Focus

This third value actively focuses on the core demands of our customers, both internal and external, to understand their needs (internal for Multinational's support functions and external for third parties.) In this way, the Multinational and its various functions rely on their capabilities and attitude to deliver products in terms of cost, quality, and deadlines.

The professional conduct expected by us implies notifying our immediate manager the moment we perceive any possibility of failing to comply with the commitment established with the client. Regardless of the underlying reason, it is critical to communicate the situation in a timely manner. Maintaining transparent and proactive communication helps to effectively manage potential challenges. In addition, it is critical to emphasize that adopting this behavior is not intended to be a superstitious expedient, such as crossing your fingers that Murphy's law chooses to take an early break during the holiday season. Rather, it is a responsible approach committed to integrity and professional ethics. The truth is that I have adopted this behavior to justify my defiance, which, although it may seem strange and silly at the same time, finds its root cause in labor laws accumulated over centuries.

Inefficient conduct, indeed. The directive was to be respected without exception, even in out-of-control events such as the loss of a loved one, where customer satisfaction was also not taken into consideration.

The Mike who was friendly and close to his teams in the early days of his position transformed into an insensitive and selfish person. Was he seeking to assert his authority over the team? Or did he simply decide to play with it? All I know is that the argument for strengthening the Multinational's cashflow by moving the rest of the days off in the current calendar year was far from consistent and efficient, especially considering that only our team had this directive. It is not a team of ten people out of 16,000 across Spain that could have a significant financial and economic impact on the Multinational, even if we shared the ten highest salaries of the Multinational headquartered in Spain.

However, in order to meet the demands of my internal clients four days before the end-of-year vacations, I had to follow another procedure established in the multinational, known as "Speak-Up". This establishes that when there is a disagreement between an employee and his or her manager, the employee must inform a manager at a higher level to obtain an impartial opinion on the situation.

I have missed fairness in this process when it became apparent. In stating my facts, Annika, Mike's manager, showed no concern. In fact, she seemed to pay no attention to me and stammered something like, "But, you know, David, maybe Mike is right and..."

"Wait, Annika," I replied, interrupting her. "I'm not here to ask you if I can enjoy my rights, but to inform you that I will not respect Mike's directive. I handle my private life very well on my own. Now tell me if this situation is going to cause problems for which I will act immediately to change my position, or if we are finally going to act like responsible adults, forget about our whims and move on."

"Oh no, no, there's no way you're leaving. And, of course, you'll move on."

"Thank you, Annika!" I said, skeptically.

So, I worked those extra days to complete my responsibilities. The effort was rewarded with genuine recognition for my work. However, that year, those congratulations had a bittersweet taste, a reflection of many years of service to a Multinational that seemed to manipulate its employees, a manipulation that contradicted the Multinational's core values. This feeling was compounded by the thought of the fundamental right that had been won through the efforts of thousands of people who had fought, even giving their lives, for one day off a year. The bitterness lessened over time, as I had finally found the impetus to consider a change of job by acting in this way, to free myself from the need to remain in my position that I had enjoyed so much until then.

The turning point in my professional career in Spain came on the day of the "Speak-Up". In part, I managed to achieve the goal I had set for myself my whole life: to have the reins well in hand to decide what I have to do or carry out in my life to be as happy as possible, even if the monkey dresses in silk, the monkey stays the same or, although golden reins do not make a horse any better. The year-end festivities passed with a mind boggled by the isolation brought on by the pandemic and the awareness that the months ahead would not be easy to manage. Then, I received Mike's annual gift to his team upon returning to work in 2021, along with the following words:

"Dear David, when we first met, I was impressed by your optimism and positivity, as well as your exemplary attitude in welcoming me. And I firmly believe that our relationship suffered the most during the Covid pandemic. We both need contact with others. Distance, Enclosure... all have a greater impact on empathetic people like you. Still, you manage the craziest projects like... our new division in Spain. Achieving these challenges requires essential trust to help each other. I promised to be closer in 2021 to align us and build that trust. I hope to see you again, stronger and longer lasting, motivating our team with your optimism.

In general, it will be fixed.

See you very soon."

This was the moment when I realized that the change was ready and underway. However, I had no idea of the spiral of events that would be unleashed over the next two and a half years.

IV.   We Are One

This value is the most representative of teamwork to break down barriers and collaborate to achieve common goals at all levels. All employees talk and listen actively with an open mind to create an inclusive workspace that promotes well-being and fun, where all employees feel part of the large family on a multinational level.

The priority level of each Multinational's function manages and negotiates the interests of customers, both internal and external, rather than local or individual interests, knowing their expectations. The objectives of each team are collectively defined and shared in line with the Multinational's priorities. Collective success takes precedence over any personal interest.

By the end of 2021, the hope of concluding such a prestigious program by early 2022 was becoming increasingly tangible. This program, eagerly awaited since negotiations began ten years ago, finally saw the light of day in early 2022. Given its dimensions, ranging from aircraft manufacturing in Spain to the installation of an assembly line in the Asian country interested in the Multinational's star product, it was necessary to carry out a complete reorganization of all departments, especially that of the Multinational's supply chain.

Although negotiations for this program began a decade ago, sales prices were not to be revised to respect the initial budgets, without taking into account the multiple crises that had occurred since then. The most significant was that caused by the COVID-19 pandemic, which resulted in a total shutdown of air traffic for two months, followed by a slow recovery in the months that followed. Despite these challenges, negotiations with the Multinational's suppliers proved challenging, though not insurmountable.

To this end, a reorganization of my team was presented to the entire Multinational with the creation of two levels of transversal positions to carry out this program. My team's objectives have been well defined and collectively shared in line with the Multinational's priorities, so that the collective success of the team takes precedence over any personal interests.

I was the only one absent from the call to define this new organization, and I only found out about its implementation at the same time as my colleagues. The surprise generated overcame any rejection that began to settle in my mind.

From "*We Are One*" I went to "*I Am One Alone*" completely distressed, not knowing what to do to denounce this discrimination I felt, and which was none other than the consequence of my refusal to enjoy my vacation entitlements on the dates the leader had decided. This feeling of singularity only increased at the beginning of spring 2023, when Patrick, our direct manager, seemed satisfied to inform his team by videoconference that the calibration of the 2022 objectives had been completed and approved by the Multinational's management, which allowed us to benefit from his financial compensation in our April payroll and therefore, all the team members had to have a personal interview with him to evaluate whether the previous year's objectives had been achieved. In the labor context of the Multinational, the annual evaluation of the objectives is a mandatory procedure established by Human Resources to review and evaluate the performance of each employee. Apparently, all the employees had their annual interview but me.

When Patrick announced that the evaluation had been done, I noticed that his attention was fixed on his camera, looking to analyze my reaction to the news. When I questioned why I had not had my assessment at the team meeting, Patrick replied that it was a personal matter and that I would receive an answer at a later time.

His smile went from ear to ear and his eyes kept glancing at each member of his team as they flicked from screen to screen in the video call. His image on my own computer screen reminded me of Alice's cat in Wonderland, frozen high above the Fantasyland maze in Park Euro Disney Park in Paris, whose eyes dart from right to left and then left to right to the infernal rhythm of a noisy, annoying Tic-Tac clock.

Five months went by, talking and trying to work things out. The only answers I received were that I did not know how to manage a project and that I could never lead a team due to my lack of skills. It is surprising when the performance of the entire implementation of a complex procurement process in the new space subsidiary of the Multinational, in a country foreign to mine, in a language foreign to mine, exceeded all expectations. These comments were disrespectful to all the effort and energy invested to make it all work.

I have never questioned my skills and competencies; rather, I have always relied on them. I already knew that in order to progress in this Multinational it was necessary to break with my principles and my values at the expense of loyal and competent collaborators. That is why I decided to stay on at the end of my probationary period in May 2009 in France, renouncing any elite position so highly valued in the corporate world. Molds do not suit me, and even less so rules dictated by ignorant and power-hungry human beings. I already realized this when, at the age of four and a half, my kindergarten teacher slapped me for kissing a boy. A situation she would have been better off keeping to herself, as it was not appreciated by my mother. It was necessary for her to teach this lady that, at my age, we did not know what kissing meant, let alone what gender the person we were kissing belonged to.

The values of the Multinational were the first ones I began to doubt, questioning whether it saw us as puppets: those who are good at hitting those who do good, without receiving blows in return. Those who were born in the 70's will remember this evil puppet, the "Guignol", who to this day remains unpunished.

Fortunately - or unfortunately - every year the Multinational imposes a mandatory virtual training for all employees in order to change mentalities and to improve the image towards our customers, who have lost confidence since the end of the first decade of the 2000's, and to ensure the well-being of each employee in the workplace.

This virtual training should be completed by the end of September. However, due to the workload until the summer vacations, I was only able to start it in August 2022 during my own vacation. The beginning of my rest period was characterized by dreary sunshine on the beach, but it was revealing to report the discrimination I had been suffering for five months.

What I didn't know - because they didn't teach it to us - is that our Human Resources department was mesmerized by the eyes of Alice's cat....

Tic...   Tic...

V.   Creativity

Creativity is about awakening curiosity, aimed at passionate, open-minded people who recognize imagination at all levels. It prepares employees to act with courage, to take and learn risks, to be able to start again if they are not met. The Multinational ensures that all employees have the time, space and tools to be creative. The most significant example of professional behavior is to create a culture that promotes the development to take assessed risks and learn from mistakes.

The virtual training is entitled "Harassment and Discrimination". In the video, the protagonist who suffers discrimination is used in an exemplary way to clearly explain how to act and how to report any case of discrimination. His story is similar to mine, being the narrative of a highly competent employee who is completely removed from his team for reasons that are unclear. His position has been filled by another employee from another department, who is in charge of performing the tasks that the discriminated employee had previously requested to carry out the implementation of the new organization of his team.

Although the new candidate undoubtedly possesses the qualities required for the position, he or she lacks the same experience and insight as the discriminated employee.

Initially, I did not pay attention to this situation, as I am not prone to mistrust and tend to believe that good gestures are adequately rewarded. Despite having accumulated almost fifty years of experience in three different countries and having lived in exotic places during my engineering fellowships that taught me otherwise, I believe in the innate goodness of people, considering myself an example of this. However, I am also aware of my cunning, especially when it comes to preserving my integrity in the face of those who act adversely towards me. Life is a challenge that I approach with determination and courage.

Faced with the discrimination I faced, it became necessary to take concrete action. This involved contacting the Ethics and Compliance department to report the facts and obtain an unbiased view of the situation. In addition, this action was aimed at reducing tensions and conflicts that could have arisen due to the discrimination.

In my first instance with the Ethics and Compliance department, I received a clear warning that dealing with this situation would not be easy. I was informed of the possibility of having to confront my manager to expose the facts. In addition, I was reminded of the importance of maintaining absolute secrecy in this process, as confidentiality was crucial to avoid possible reprisals from my manager if he disapproved of the investigation.

Confidentiality, in my case, was only partially maintained. Initially, I did not see the sense in keeping it confidential, considering the training we had received. However, as my discomfort grew in the following months due to the lack of protective measures from the Multinational, I decided to seek psychological help and contacted the Hotline of the

Multinational (although this word sounds impressive, in reality, it is not effective in practice.) Today, I am still searching for answers.

The investigation, which lasted nine long months, finally determined that my situation was not discriminatory in any way. In the last video call concluding the investigation, the manager of the colleague in charge of my case explained why it was not considered discriminatory, basing her arguments on the training we had received. I went so far as to question her as to whether we had gone through the same training, to which she affirmed that we had.

Surprisingly, however, she argued that my interpretation was not correct because of my mastery of Spanish in such a short time. It was then that I reminded her that I had been trained in French, the language in which I am most fluent of the four that I use, speak and write on a daily basis.

The situation left me with no expectation of a coherent response from her.

I was not mistaken.

VI.   Reliability

Reliability is responsible for the unprecedented success of this Multinational. It takes personal responsibility for its actions and commitments to its employees to deliver innovative and gravity-defying products, on time, while reducing its costs to satisfy its customers and valuing its employees for their skills, enabling them to live comfortably through remuneration significantly above the national average of any country where it is implemented.

To achieve this, the Multinational must act consistently when mistakes are made and learn not to repeat them, especially when it intends to publicly demonstrate its commitment to a better reputation and correct past mistakes that could affect customer loyalty. However, this statement is far from reflecting reality. The evidence for this lies in its behavior in response to my actions aimed at respecting the stated values. In fact, despite following and applying the mandatory learning that the Multinational promotes, the achievement of my objectives was poorly perceived by it, as it was not aligned with the behavior taught to its collaborators, ultimately.

The failure of reliability at the Multinational was evident as soon as it was implemented. Since 2017, the Individual Salary Review (ISR) of each employee had been defined by a point system based on 4 criteria: achievement of annual objectives, salary situation, seniority in the Multinational and Manager's assessment. The TOP45 selected 45% of the best performers to qualify for the ISR. Despite my presence in the TOP45 in 2017, I did not benefit from it. When I claimed it to Human Resources, the following week, without any explanation, they changed upwards the total of points that gave right to the ISR in view of my result and thus depriving me of the opportunity to obtain it.

Just two days before the start of my long-awaited vacation to enjoy the April Fair in Seville, in April 2023, a colleague from the Human Resources department summoned me to hand-deliver a letter of dismissal, alleging severe reasons and demanding that I account for my actions within a period of only seventy-two hours, which was equivalent to the following weekend. At the time, I did not stop to verify the legality of this summons, to tell the truth. My reaction was one of deep disappointment upon receiving this notification.

After fourteen and a half years dedicated to what I do best in my life, both professionally and personally, I found myself facing a dismissal under the pretext of incompetence and fraud for fictitious work. This unexpected turn of events was especially painful, as I remembered with gratitude the person who had given me the opportunity to come to Spain and live my life as a citizen of the world, supporting the idea that I was the right person in the right place. His comment had touched me deeply at the time, as it was the first one that gave me the confidence I so desperately needed in my life. It came from someone who believed in me, marking a significant contrast to my family, who early in my life never supported my choices because of their belief in my inability. It was painful to realize the extent to which homophobia affected my parents, going so far as to tell me that I would never find a job because of my sexual orientation.

As a result of these circumstances, the first three years of my professional career involved facing extremely difficult challenges. Although I had foreseen these difficulties, I decided to accept the first job offer as a salesman that came after I finished my engineering degree, which led me to sell the product I did not believe in, as I mentioned at the beginning of this autobiography. I did it not only for myself, but also to prove to those who loved me deeply that homosexuality should not be considered a disgrace in life. Despite the challenges, the outcome was not as negative as could have been expected, although I faced financial difficulties in 2003 because of this choice. I did everything, then, in my power to change my situation and pursue my true passions, convinced that happiness can only be found by being authentic and true to oneself. I do not believe that we can be truly happy by pretending to be someone we are not.

As this complicated period recurred once again in my life, I found a fundamental difference between the two: in this latest episode, the adversity was simply a consequence of my commitment to my values and beliefs. However, my confidence in these values reaffirmed the solidity of my integrity. I would certainly opt for dismissal rather than stay in an environment that did not align with my true principles, even though I had initially come to Spain in search of comfort and financial stability.

I was half wrong.

VII.   Integrity

Integrity is a value and a state that makes it possible to preserve the qualities and original state of individuals without alteration.

Faced with the summons from Human Resources that I received two days before my April 2023 vacation, related to the issue of "fictitious work," I chose to remain silent, as I found no reason to justify any action of the one that occurred and which is developed below. However, this decision triggered a second summons, in which I was notified of my immediate dismissal for serious cause.

In fact, during my period of depression which was only the consequence of the accumulation of all these events, I had asked my direct manager for the possibility of working from home, although this request was not formalized in writing. To account for my working hours, I began to manually enter my schedules into the Multinational's attendance control system. However, what I did not know at that time was that there was a double attendance register: the first one when entering the facilities, either pedestrian or vehicular, and the second one when entering the office, with readers installed at each access to the Multinational's factory buildings to verify our presence.

Human Resources does not inform employees of the first clock-in record, which gives them the ability to verify whether the employee showed up at the office, as indicated by the time and attendance system. Manual entries in the attendance system could be misinterpreted as fictitious work. However, I underline the verbal term "being able to define" because the reality is quite the opposite. I have never in my life put in so many hours of uninterrupted work while working from home. Contrary to what we might think, even before the legalization of teleworking in Spain, I never received any compensation for the additional hours of work realized in my office since my integration eight years ago, nor did I seek to be remunerated.

What would be my incentive to carry out a fictitious job if, in the end, there was no reward or even the slightest recognition? What a good idiot I would be!

It seems that the Multinational has found a way to fire its employees at its own discretion, regardless of the circumstances. This goes against the values that the Multinational proclaims, such as Integrity and Respect, and demonstrates a disconnection with the reality of the employees who have dedicated years of effort to the Multinational.

It is crucial that companies maintain integrity and transparency in their policies and processes, especially on issues related to attendance and working time. Homework and time management can pose challenges, and a lack of communication or understanding of procedures can lead to misunderstandings. It is essential that companies address these issues in a fair and transparent manner, clearly communicating to their employees what the procedures and expectations are regarding attendance and timekeeping.

I remember the words of a former French colleague who told me that companies compensate us for the use of our brainpower. I agree with this statement, but it is important to emphasize that the use of our intellectual abilities is personal and must be under our control. When we give up our mental capacity solely for economic reasons, we could compare it to prostituting our talent, which is unacceptable in the workplace.

However, as I always say to myself, every situation has its positive side. It was the first time I met the head of Human Resources in Spain, an individual who rarely, if ever, appears unless a problematic situation arises. Although I do not remember his name, I am sure he will remember mine for the rest of his life. This is because, somehow, my situation challenged him.

I consider this an achievement, at least in part. I am grateful that he confirmed my suspicions as to whether the Multinational's Management was aware of the situation. The answer turned out to be negative because he did not answer my direct question, which sheds light on the lack of attention of top management to the real problems affecting their employees.

I wanted to find out so that I could tell them that the procedure they have implemented is not effective and never will be. This is largely because the people responsible for judging the fairness of a situation have lost their objectivity due to their long tenure in their positions, which in some cases exceeds two or three decades. It is true that experience is valuable, but in this case, it does not apply. Soups stay richer when cooked in old pots, but it is not the old pots that can change a recipe.

What makes this situation even more pathetic is that my dismissal occurred without the presence of my direct managers and without prior communication from them, which confirms the non-relationship they have had with me for the past three years.

It is interesting to note that human psychology sometimes leads us to seek comfort solutions when faced with difficult situations. These solutions can carry with them psychological and moral blackmail, as victims often fear losing their current comfort. However, we are all different in the way we cope with these circumstances. Personally, I would rather sleep peacefully under a bridge than spend sleepless nights living a life that does not satisfy me.

This autobiography does not seek to be vindictive nor is it intended to denounce the dishonesty of the Multinational. Instead, it is intended to define my concept of integrity. It is the point of view that allows me to live a happy and serene life.

In the past, I did not believe that it was possible to find happiness in life, as there always seemed to be something that disturbed it in daily life. However, I have changed my mind. I now know that living happily involves making choices and struggling to enforce situations that are not always under our control. When we value ourselves as we wish to be valued, new opportunities open up for us. Some people argue that heaven is not earned without effort, and this is true for many. However, some have achieved their goals by sacrificing others and offering them the opportunity to explore the world we live in, sometimes even passing on pandemics that affected regions we did not even imagine opening up to the world.

I could be called brave and admirable for following my own path and making choices that reflect my true identity and values. Being true to oneself and pursuing authenticity are essential to finding happiness and fulfillment in life. Despite the challenges and difficulties, we often face on that path, in the end, living in accordance with our values and being honest with ourselves is a reward in itself.

Many of us are right.

My Integrity is the pillar of my serenity and no one can take it away from me.

"Don't forget that we invented the machine to travel in time and space and to other worlds: the book. Read on."

Maxime Chattam

Enter my world by following my Social Networks: